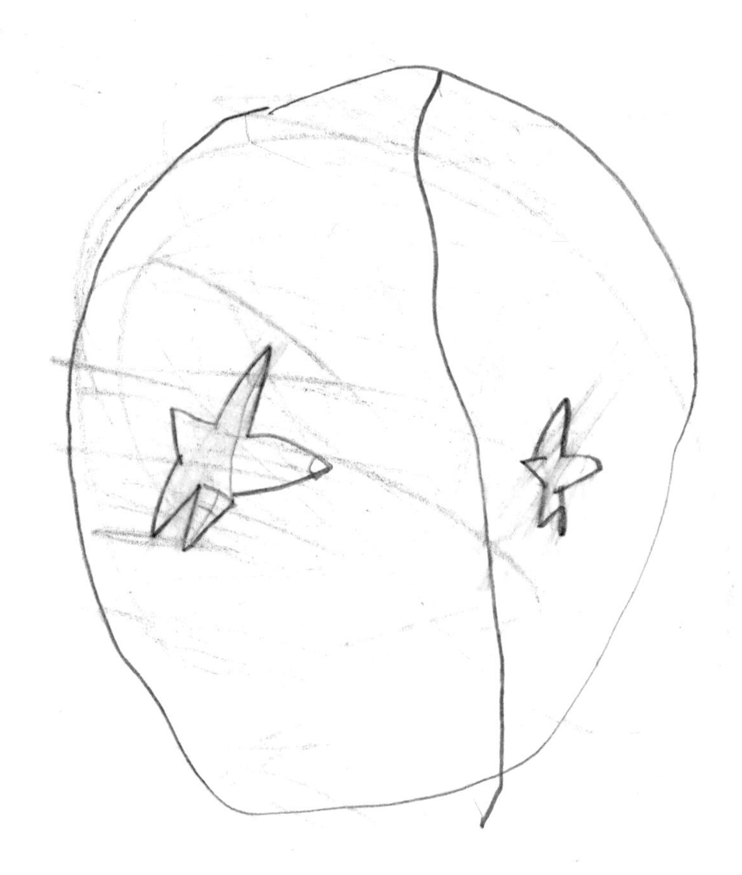

Sports Math

The Math of Soccer

Ian F. Mahaney

PowerKiDS press
New York

For Brenda

Published in 2012 by The Rosen Publishing Group, Inc.
29 East 21st Street, New York, NY 10010

First Edition

Editor: Joanne Randolph
Layout Design: Greg Tucker

Photo Credits: Cover Laurence Griffiths/Getty Images; pp. 4–5, 5 (right), 7 (right), 10–11, 12 (left), 12–13, 14 (left) Shutterstock.com; pp. 6–7 Pulsar Imagens/Delfim Martins/Getty Images; p. 8 (left) Christof Koepsel/Bongarts/Getty Images; pp. 8–9 Jamie Squire/FIFA via Getty Images; pp. 14–15 Sari Gustafsson/AFP/Getty Images; pp. 16–17 Michael Steele/Getty Images; pp. 18–19 Christian Petersen/Getty Images; p. 20 (left) Paul Gilham/Getty Images; pp. 20–21 Roberto Schmidt/AFP/Getty Images.

Library of Congress Cataloging-in-Publication Data

Mahaney, Ian F.
The math of soccer / by Ian F. Mahaney. — 1st ed.
p. cm. — (Sports math)
Includes index.
ISBN 978-1-4488-2557-8 (library binding) — ISBN 978-1-4488-2700-8 (pbk.) —
ISBN 978-1-4488-2701-5 (6-pack)
1. Soccer—Mathematics—Juvenile literature. 2. Arithmetic—Juvenile literature. I. Title.
GV943.25.M24 2012
796.3340151—dc22

2010030043

Manufactured in the United States of America

CPSIA Compliance Information: Batch #WW11PK: For Further Information contact Rosen Publishing, New York, New York at 1-800-237-9932

Contents

How Does Soccer Work? 4
Fields and Sizes 6
Take Your Time! 8
About the Ball 10
Goalie Math 12
Taking the Shot 14
Soccer Stats 16
The Standings 18
The World Cup 20
Figure It Out: The Answers 22
Glossary 23
Index 24
Web Sites 24

How Does Soccer Work?

Soccer is a sport in which two teams try to kick a small ball into the other team's **goal**. The object is to score more goals than the other team.

Each team has 11 players on the field. Players can use their feet, legs, chests, and heads to move the ball. In most

Landon Donovan (left) of the United States tries to get the ball away from Australian player Mark Bresciano (right).

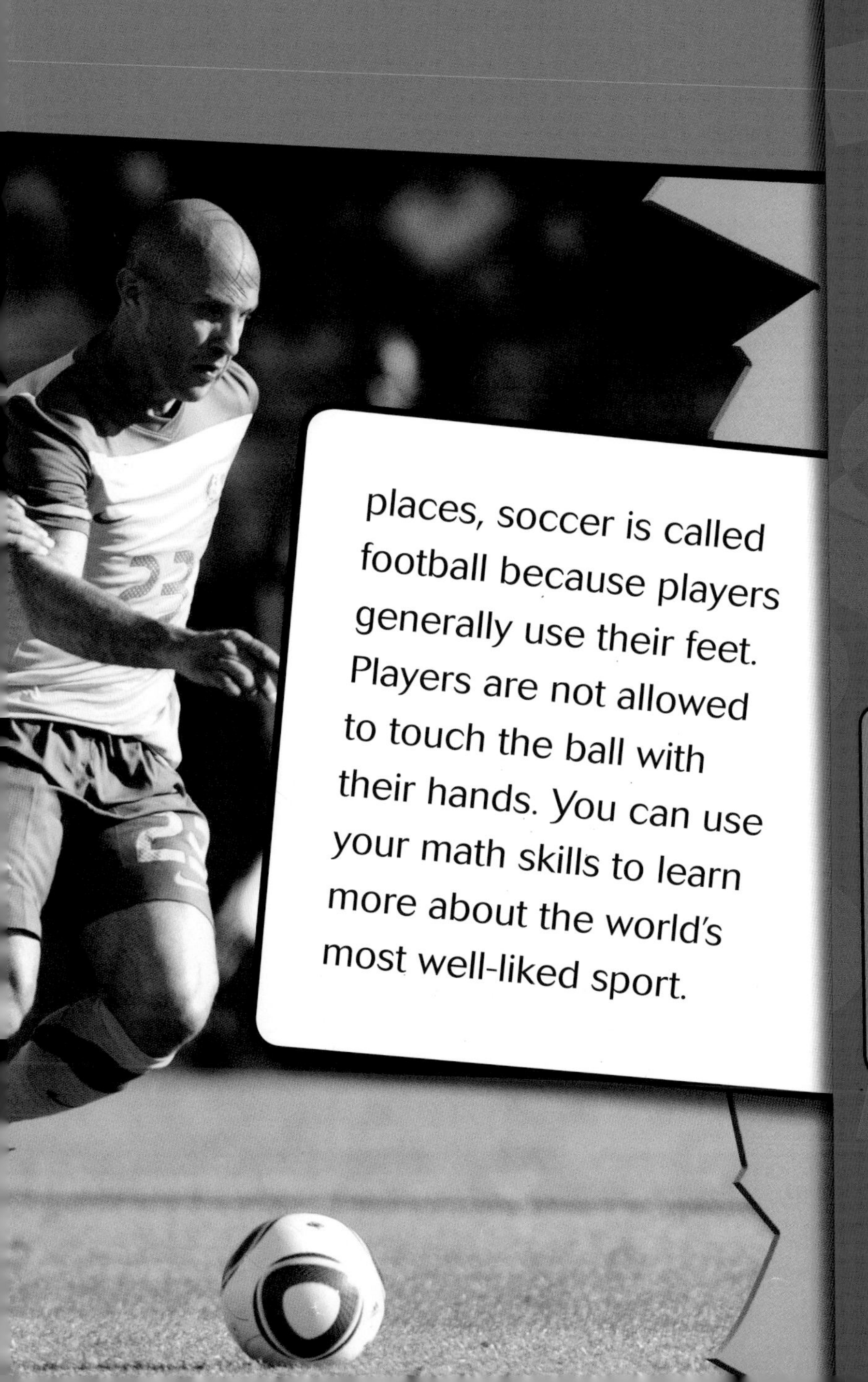

places, soccer is called football because players generally use their feet. Players are not allowed to touch the ball with their hands. You can use your math skills to learn more about the world's most well-liked sport.

Figure It Out!

The goalie is 1 of the 11 players on the field. The goalie guards the goal. The goalie is the only player allowed to touch the ball with her hands. How many players on the field cannot touch the ball with their hands?

(See page 22 for the answers.)

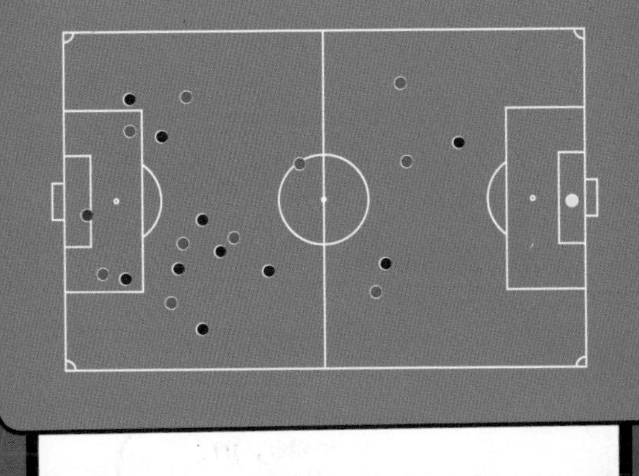

Fields and Sizes

Soccer is played on a **rectangular** field. Different fields are not always the same **length** and **width**. The length of a soccer field must always be greater than the width, though. The size depends on the event and the age of the players. FIFA is the group that runs international soccer. FIFA's fields are measured in meters. They must be between 45 and 90 meters (148–295 ft) wide and between 90 and 120 meters (295–394 ft) long.

Soccer players that play on FIFA fields run over 6 miles (10 km) in a game.

There is a line in the center that divides the field into two equal halves. On each end of the field, there is a goal. Each team defends one of the goals.

Figure It Out!

If you play on a soccer field that is 80 yards (73 m) long and 50 yards (46 m) wide, how much longer is the field than it is wide? What is the length of half the field?

(See page 22 for the answers.)

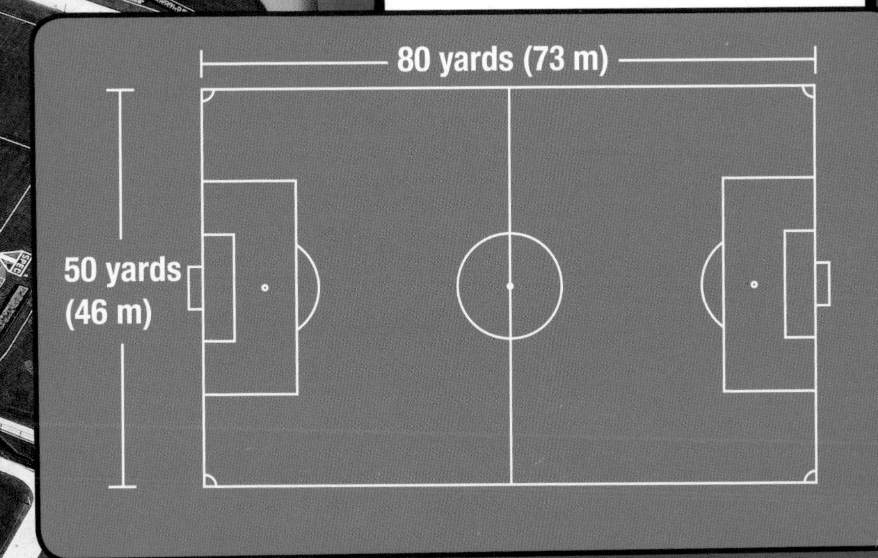

Take Your Time!

FIFA soccer games are played in two time segments, called halves. Each half is 45 minutes long. To find out how long a whole game is, you can write a math **equation**:

45 minutes + 45 minutes = 90 minutes.

This scoreboard shows the amount of time played at the top. If this is a 90-minute game, how much time is left?

Some **leagues** with younger players play four quarters in a game. Say a game has four quarters, and each quarter is 12 minutes long. The equation to find the length of the whole game would be:

4×12 minutes
= 48 minutes.

Another way to write this is:

12 minutes + 12 minutes
+ 12 minutes + 12 minutes
= 48 minutes.

In FIFA games, the teams sometimes play into extra time if the game is tied after 90 minutes. The teams can play two 15-minute periods of extra time to find a winner. What is the longest a FIFA game can be?

(See page 22 for the answers.)

In some games a penalty shoot-out may be used if a game is still tied after extra time.

About the Ball

There are three sizes of balls used in soccer games. Size 5 is used in FIFA games. The chart below shows you the sizes that children and adults use. It also shows you the weight and circumference of each ball.

Size	Approximate Ages	Circumference	Weight
3	Under 8	23–24 inches (58–61 cm)	11–12 ounces (310–340 g)
4	9–12	25–26 inches (63.5–66 cm)	12–13 ounces (340–368.5 g)
5	12 and up	27–28 inches (69–71 cm)	14–16 ounces (397–454 g)

The circumference is the measurement around the ball. To find the circumference, wrap a piece of string around the ball and measure the string with a ruler.

Lighter, smaller soccer balls are used by younger people so that they can control the ball better.

Figure It Out!

Let's try to read the chart on the facing page. What size ball would a team of 14-year-olds use? How much does that ball weigh?

(See page 22 for the answers.)

Goalie Math

The goalie defends a goal that is 8 feet (2.4 m) tall and 24 feet (7 m) wide. That is a large space for one person to defend. The goalie does many things that help him defend that space. The goalie watches the ball and his opponents to see where the ball is going and how fast. He is using lots of math without even knowing it!

Staying Back

Moving Forward

This picture makes it easy to see how a goalie can cut off the angle by moving toward the shooter.

The goalie can defend more of the goal by moving toward the person shooting the ball. When a goalie moves toward the shooter, this is called cutting off the **angle**. This makes it harder for the shooter to make a shot on goal.

Being a goalie is hard! He has to judge where the ball is going and then get there quickly!

Figure It Out!

Younger players use smaller goals. The smallest goal used in games is 4 feet (1 m) high and 6 feet (2 m) long. How much larger is the goal that adults use?

(See page 22 for the answers.)

Taking the Shot

Goalies are not the only ones using angles in soccer. The offense uses them, too. If an offensive player can see more of the goal, it is easier for her to score.

Say the goalie and other defensive players are blocking one player's view of the goal. That player can pass the ball to a teammate with a better angle. The player with a better angle

A

B

The goalie has moved toward player A to block his shot on the goal. Player B has a much better view of the goal. If A passes to B, their team has a better chance of scoring!

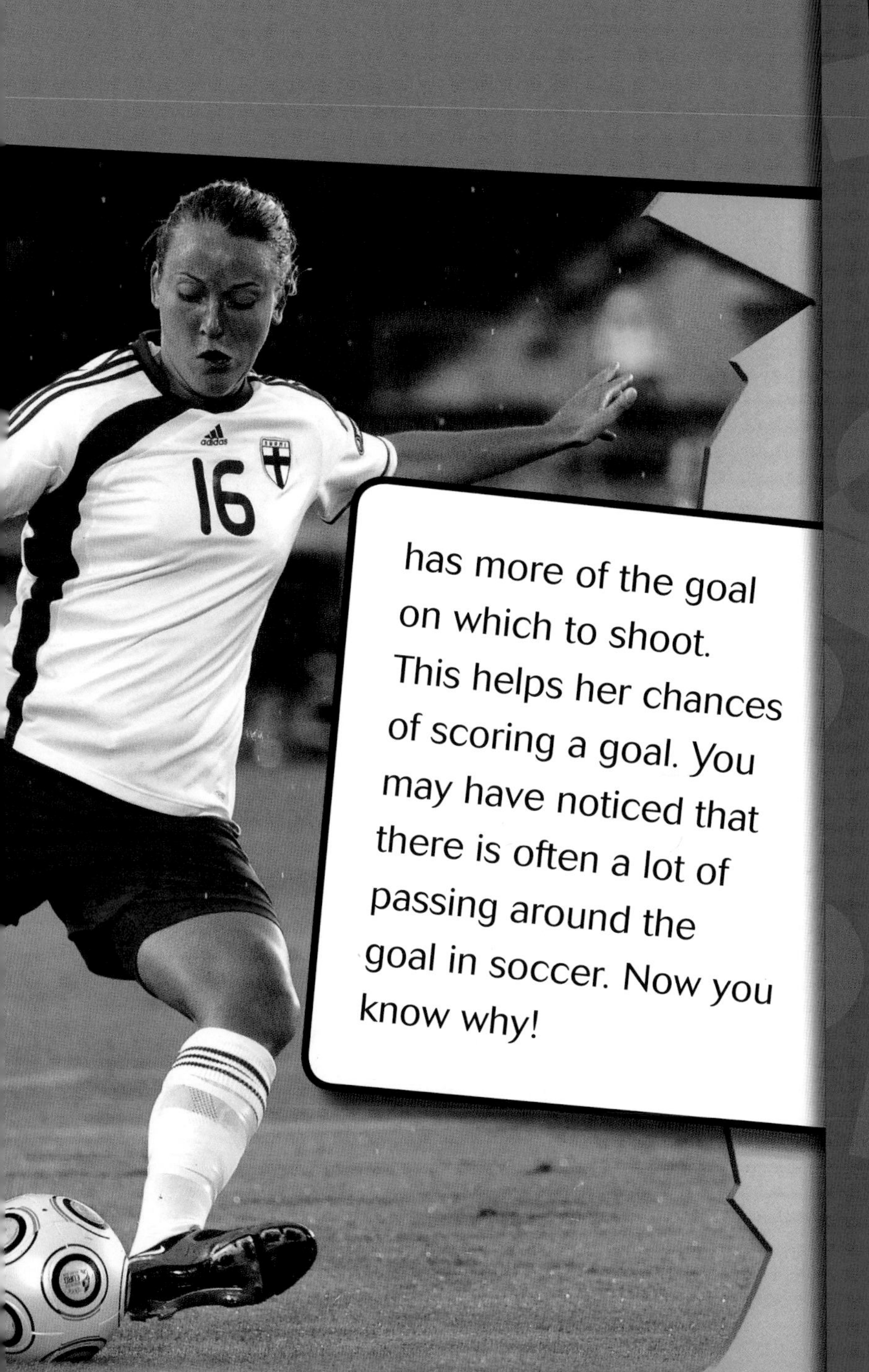

has more of the goal on which to shoot. This helps her chances of scoring a goal. You may have noticed that there is often a lot of passing around the goal in soccer. Now you know why!

Figure It Out!

Spain is playing Paraguay, and the game is still tied after extra time. When this happens in some soccer games, there is a **penalty shoot-out.** Each team has five chances to score. If Spain makes three of five kicks, what **percentage** of kicks has Spain made?

(See page 22 for the answers.)

Soccer Stats

Statistics, or stats, is the study of groups of numbers in order to compare things. Fans, coaches, and players look at many numbers to help them understand how good a player is.

Most statistics in soccer count things. The number of goals a player has and the number of shots a player has taken are examples of counting statistics.

In his 2009–2010 season with the Portuguese national team, Óscar Cardozo had a shooting percentage of 59.5%.

Shooting percentage helps us understand how good a player is at scoring goals. FIFA calls shooting percentage the goals per shot rate. To find a player's shooting percentage, divide the number of goals a player scored by the number of tries she made.

Figure It Out!

If Wesley takes 22 shots and makes 5 of them, what is his shooting percentage?

(See page 22 for the answers.)

The Standings

Most soccer teams are in a league. Major League Soccer is a professional league in the United States and Canada.

The Los Angeles Galaxy is often at the top of the standings.

In MLS, when a team wins a game, it earns three points. When a team ties a game, it earns one point. The team does not earn points if it loses a game. Each team's points are added together. The teams are then ranked, from the best to the worst, by the number of points they have. This ranking is called the standings.

Figure It Out!

This chart has the numbers of wins, losses, and ties of each team that plays in MLS's Western **Conference**. Can you sort them by number of points, from first place down?

Team	W	L	T
Real Salt Lake	8	3	3
FC Dallas	5	2	6
Chivas USA	3	9	2
Colorado Rapids	6	3	4
Houston Dynamo	5	7	3
Seattle Sounders FC	4	8	3
Los Angeles Galaxy	11	1	3
San Jose Earthquakes	5	4	4

(See page 22 for the answers.)

The World Cup

The FIFA World Cup is a **tournament** of the world's best men's soccer teams. It happens every four years. There is also a FIFA Women's World Cup every four years.

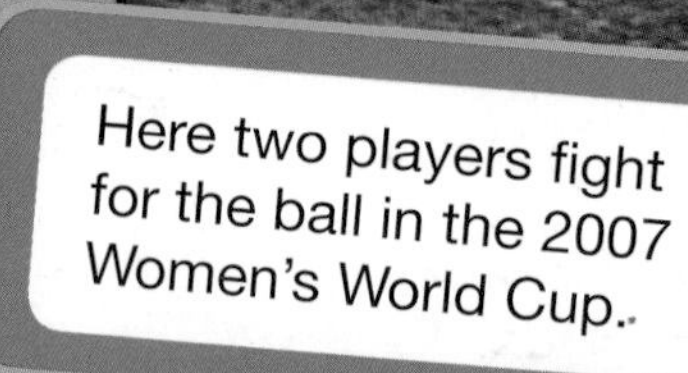

Here two players fight for the ball in the 2007 Women's World Cup.

In the first round of the World Cup, 32 teams play. Half of the teams, or $32 \div 2 = 16$, are **eliminated**. The other half moves on to the next round.

There are five rounds in the World Cup. In each round, half the teams are eliminated. The last game is the final. Two teams are left to play in this match and the winner is the champion.

Andrés Iniesta, in blue, of Spain scores the first goal in extra time during the 2010 World Cup final game against the Netherlands.

Figure It Out!

The Women's World Cup starts with 16 teams. In each round, half the teams are eliminated. How many rounds are needed to crown a champion?
Hint: **A chart will help you.**

(See page 22 for the answers.)

Figure It Out: The Answers

Page 5: 11 – 1 = 10 players who cannot touch the ball with their hands on one team. 10 players x 2 teams = 20 players on the field who cannot use their hands.

Page 7: The field is 80 yards – 50 yards = 30 yards longer than it is wide. Half the field is 80 yards ÷ 2 = 40 yards long.

Page 9: The longest a FIFA game can be is 90 minutes + 15 minutes + 15 minutes = 120 minutes = 2 hours.

Page 11: A team of 14-year-olds would use a size 5 ball, which weighs 14–16 ounces (397–454 g).

Page 13: A goal used in an adult game is 24 feet – 6 feet = 18 feet wider. An adult goal is 8 feet – 4 feet = 4 feet taller.

Page 15: Spain makes (3 ÷ 5) x 100 = 0.6 x 100 = 60% of its kicks.

Page 17: Wesley's shooting percentage is (5 ÷ 22) x 100 = (0.23) x 100 = 23%.

Page 19:

	Points	W	L	T
Los Angeles Galaxy	36	11	1	3
Real Salt Lake	27	8	3	3
Colorado Rapids	22	6	3	4
FC Dallas	21	5	2	6
San Jose Earthquakes	19	5	4	4
Houston Dynamo	18	5	7	3
Seattle Sounders FC	15	4	8	3
Chivas USA	11	3	9	2

Page 21: It takes four rounds to find a champion. Here is a chart to help you see how to find this answer:

Round Number	Teams Playing in This Round	Teams Eliminated	Teams Advancing to Next Round
1	16	8	8
2	8	4	4
3	4	2	2
4	2	1	

Glossary

angle (ANG-gul) The space between two lines that come together at a point.

conference (KON-feh-rents) A grouping of sports teams.

eliminated (ih-LIH-muh-nayt-ed) Removed.

equation (ih-KWAY-zhun) A math statement that says that two different things are equal.

goal (GOHL) The place where a player puts the ball to score a point.

leagues (LEEGZ) Groups of teams that play one another.

length (LENGTH) The measure of how long something is.

penalty shoot-out (PEH-nul-tee SHOOT-owt) When each soccer team is given five free chances to score a goal.

percentage (per-SEN-tij) One part of 100.

rectangular (rek-TAN-gyoo-lur) Having four straight sides and four square corners. Two of the sides are longer than two of the other sides.

tournament (TOR-nuh-ment) A group of games to decide the best team.

width (WITH) The measure of how wide something is.

Index

A
angle(s), 13–14

B
ball(s), 4–5, 10–14

E
equation, 8–9

F
field, 4–7
FIFA, 6, 17

G
game(s), 8–10, 13, 15, 18, 21
goalie(s), 5, 12–14
goal(s), 4–5, 7, 12–17

H
halves, 7–8

L
league(s), 9, 18
length, 6–7, 9
line, 7

O
object, 4

P
penalty shoot-out, 15
percentage, 15, 17
player(s), 4–6, 9, 13–14, 16–17

Q
quarter(s), 9

S
skills, 5
sport, 4–5

T
team(s), 4, 7, 9, 11, 15, 18–21
tournament, 20

W
Western Conference, 19
width, 6

Web Sites

Due to the changing nature of Internet links, PowerKids Press has developed an online list of Web sites related to the subject of this book. This site is updated regularly. Please use this link to access the list:
www.powerkidslinks.com/sm/soccer/